DEDICATION

This book is dedicated to all of the young girls and boys who love math and science. May your curiosity and passion guide you to become the engineers and scientists who shape our future.

Many years ago, there was a little boy named **Miles**. He was in first grade and **loved** going to school every day.

Miles's favorite class was **math**. He **loved** numbers! While other kids played with toys, Miles played with numbers.

One day, the teacher wrote a **tricky** problem on the board. Miles's hand shot up! He **knew** the answer right away.

"Great job, Miles!" said the teacher. "You have a **real** talent for math!" Miles felt proud and happy.

In **middle school**, Miles joined the **math club**. He met other kids who loved math as much as he did.

They practiced hard for competitions, especially the big National **MATHCOUNTS**® competition. Miles felt ready to take on the challenge.

At the competition, Miles solved problem after problem. His heart **raced** as he waited for the results.

Miles didn't win first place, but he scored high and learned that hard work and **teamwork** are what **truly** matter.

In high school, math became even **more** challenging, but Miles was ready. He took **advanced** classes and **loved** learning new things.

Miles also joined the **robotics** club, where he could use math to build cool **machines** with his friends.

Balancing math, robotics, and other activities **wasn't** easy, but Miles kept going. He **knew** he was preparing for a bright future.

By the end of high school, Miles earned a **scholarship** to study engineering in **college**. His hard work was paying off!

Miles started college with **excitement**. He **loved** his engineering classes and enjoyed solving real-world problems.

He joined engineering clubs and worked on **projects** like building a model bridge with his friends.

College was **challenging**, but Miles knew he was getting closer to becoming an engineer. He studied hard and **never** gave up.

After years of hard work, Miles **graduated** with his engineering degree. His family was so proud of him!

After college, Miles got his first job as an **engineer**. He was excited to start working on **real** projects.

Miles worked hard and learned a lot from his experienced colleagues. He helped **design** a community park, and he loved seeing his ideas come to **life**.

Seeing the finished park filled with happy families made Miles feel **proud**. He knew he was making a **difference**.

After a few years, Miles decided to take the Professional Engineer (PE) Exam. It was a big **challenge**, but he was ready.

After **months** of studying, Miles was ready to take the PE Exam. It was the **biggest** test of his life.

The exam was **tough**, but Miles stayed calm and used **everything** he had learned over the years.

When the results came in, Miles was **overjoyed**. He had passed! He was now a **Professional Engineer**!

Miles's family was so **proud** of him. They **knew** he would do great things as a Professional Engineer.

Miles's family gathered for a special dinner to **celebrate** his success. They shared **stories** about how Miles loved math from a young age.

Grandpa shared a story about how little Miles used to count **everything**, from his toys to the stars in the sky.

Miles thanked his family for their support. He **knew** he couldn't have done it without them.

As the night ended, Miles felt grateful and excited for the future. He knew his **journey** was just beginning.

As the years passed, Miles became an **experienced** engineer, and he knew it was time to **give back**. He joined a professional society to help other engineers.

He attended meetings and shared his knowledge with **younger** engineers, helping them **grow** in their careers.

Miles also taught courses, passing on everything he had learned over the years. He **loved** seeing young engineers succeed.

Miles knew that by giving back, he was helping to **build** a brighter future for the **next** generation of engineers.

So, do **YOU** like Math? If so, maybe you can become an Engineer one day - because the World **needs** more Engineers! Miles hopes you'll follow your passion and make a difference by becoming a Professional Engineer!

ABOUT THE AUTHOR

David Janover, PE, is a professional engineer with over 30 years of experience in civil engineering. He has served as the Chair of the Order of the Engineer from 2022 to 2024, advocating for the ethical practice of engineering. A passionate advocate for education and the engineering profession, David has dedicated his career to public service and mentoring young engineers, inspiring the next generation through his writing. He holds degrees from The Cooper Union, New York City, and has been actively involved in engineering societies, always striving to give back to the community and the profession. David's love for math and engineering is matched only by his commitment to helping others achieve their dreams in the field.

www.ingramcontent.com/pod-product-compliance
Lightning Source LLC
LaVergne TN
LVHW080528210926
848481LV00022B/3646
* 9 7 9 8 2 9 5 5 0 2 3 6 1 *

Miles Ahead:

A Journey in Math and Engineering

ISBN: 9798336848557